pasta

Written by Christine Smith

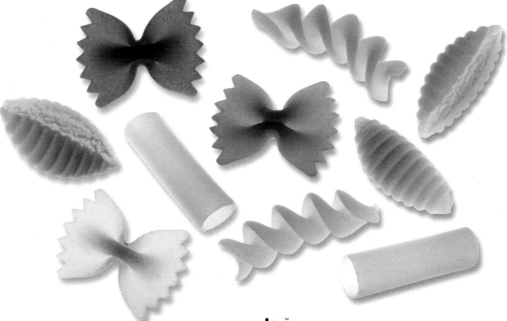

TOP THAT!
PUBLISHING PLC

Published by Top That! Publishing plc
Tide Mill Way, Woodbridge, Suffolk, IP12 1AP, UK
www.topthatpublishing.com
Copyright © 2010 Top That! Publishing plc

Contents

Contents

Our Love Affair with Pasta

Pasta has rapidly found its place in our kitchens as a true staple. It is the perfect store cupboard food and lends itself to endless variations of tastes, flavors, textures and colors. It can be used to make the simplest of satisfying dishes or to create more extravagant, complex recipes. Its versatility makes it excellent for soups and salads, as well as with lots of different sauces to create delicious main courses.

In Italy, people are used to eating pasta every day, and it is produced in a great number of different types, shapes and flavors.

Dried pasta is used on a daily basis, although fresh pasta is very popular and available from most grocery stores and delicatessens, as well as being quite easy to make yourself.

Ready-made pasta dishes can be found in chiller cabinets and freezer compartments in most grocery stores and there are lots of freeze-dried pasta varieties on the shelves. In fact, pasta is everywhere—so is it any wonder that many of us are beginning to take after the Italians and eat it several times a week?

Pasta is popular because of its widespread appeal—even a novice cook can use it to create a good, simple meal. Many dishes are very quickly prepared. It is a low fat food, which is both delicious and satisfying when combined with a tasty sauce.

The recipes featured in this book all serve four people as a main course or 6–8 people if served as a side dish.

A Little History

Pasta has been around for centuries, and existed in the country now known as Italy long before it was brought back by explorers from the East.

At times in Italian history, pasta has been a food of the poor—a peasant food made from flour and water, that was filling and sustaining. At other times, however, some forms of pasta were found only on the tables of the rich—especially in dishes like ravioli and lasagne, where an egg-based pasta was combined with rich sauces or stuffed with tasty fillings.

Spaghetti goes back a long way and was one of the first pastas to be made industrially in Italy, where it was hung over long poles to dry. Large pasta plants have existed there since the end of the 19th century, and by the early years of the 20th century, large high speed presses were producing the ridged, twisted and curved shapes that we have become used to today. Although people liked to make pasta at home, in many households buying factory-made spaghetti soon superceded the daily process of pasta making.

Beyond Italy

Pasta is a dough made up of flour and water, sometimes with egg added for flavor and richness. Variations on this simple combination are found throughout history across a range of different cultures.

In China and Japan, for example, noodles have been part of the cuisine for hundreds of years, often made from non-wheat flours: buckwheat, rice, potato and mung bean flours are common, along with unusual flavorings such as green tea.

Stuffed pasta is also found in these countries—the Chinese make steamed dumplings, and in Japan an unusual sweet ravioli is made using strawberry flavored rice dough stuffed with sweetened adzuki beans.

The making of Cantonese noodles is an art form perfected over centuries of tradition, handed down through the generations. These noodles—so fine that they can pass through the eye of a large needle—are made solely by hand, the individual strands emerging through many processes of stretching, twisting and folding.

Recently pasta has spread into many other countries. In Greece there are many different types of pasta used in cooking. It is often served as an accompaniment to other foods—spaghetti is a very popular choice. In soups, a tiny pasta called orzo which looks like grains of rice is very popular. The Greeks also make a baked pasta dish, rather like lasagne, called pastitsio.

In Germany, spaetzle is made by extruding a soft pasta dough through a special press held over a pan of boiling water. The Polish and Russian people have pierogi—little steamed parcels stuffed with vegetables, meat or fruit. However, it is the Italians who have been central to the export of their national dish worldwide and it is their pasta that is celebrated in this book.

Different Types of Pasta

There are many different types of pasta available from shops and delicatessens in the US. Fresh egg pasta is sold in vacuum packs and also comes sold stuffed as ravioli and tortellini. Depending on their quality, these can be excellent, or limp and tasteless. When buying this type of pasta look for an Italian shop which produces its own and sells it loose—this will be much nearer to the fresh pasta you can make at home.

For pure convenience, and often flavor as well, it is generally easier to buy dried pasta to use at home. There are now so many different sorts: basic spaghetti and other simple shapes like fusilli made from durum semolina wheat; dried egg pasta often made into tagliatelle and fettuccine, and those lovely broad noodles called pappardelle. Rustic pastas that are dried slowly, having been made into traditional recipes like orecchiette from Puglia, or malloreddus from Sardinia.

It is easy to find lots of different colored and flavored pastas, which you can make at home. Squid ink pasta has become very fashionable, with its black color provided by the addition of squid ink before the dough is shaped. The addition of spinach or broccoli will create green pasta, while red indicates added tomato, and yellow, added saffron. Pasta also comes flavored with mushrooms, herbs, garlic or chili.

7

Using Pasta

Faced with the wonderful array of pastas available, from even a modest grocery store, it is useful to have some idea of how to choose and use them.

Many dishes involve coating the pasta in a particular sauce, and it is important, as well as fun, to match the pasta with the sauce. Long thin pastas, like spaghetti and linguine, seem to go well with oily sauces, as well as light sauces like those made from little shellfish. Chunky pastas and those with holes and folds, like rigatoni, conchiglie and penne, are best with chunky, robust sauces, which would simply slide off thin strands. There are also pastas which are suitable to use in soups—little shapes like anellini and conchigliette, very thin strands like capellini, often called "angel hair", and vermicelli. Noodles, such as pappardelle and fettuccine, make superb side dishes simply coated with a little butter or olive oil and can be served with all manner of main courses.

However, don't get too worried about what goes with what—above all, you should enjoy using the different pastas you find in whatever way you like.

Key Ingredients

Flour

The best flour for making your own pasta is original Italian type 00 flour. You can mix this with semolina flour, also called durum wheat flour, to make a more earthy, slightly rough, pasta. Ordinary plain flour, suitable for bread making, can be used but cake-making flour is too low in gluten and will not make a dough that is elastic and stretchy. Wholemeal flour makes a heavier, nuttier pasta, although this is rarely found in Italy.

Salt

An important ingredient in pasta making, salt helps the dough to become elastic and adds flavor. Use finely ground sea salt whenever possible. Salt is also often added to the cooking water to help flavor the pasta.

Olive Oil

This is a staple of Italian pasta cookery, whether added to homemade pasta dough to add sheen, elasticity and flavor, or used to coat cooked pasta before serving it. A good quality, extra virgin olive oil is great to use for coating pasta as it will impart a wonderful, rich earthiness to the dish. However, if you are cooking with olive oil, a lighter second pressing oil will be best. It can be a mistake to heat extra virgin oils to a high temperature as the oil can denature and the flavor will be spoilt. Keep special oils for dressings, coating hot pasta or for drizzling over the finished dish before serving.

Key Ingredients

Tomatoes

A key ingredient in Italian cooking, tomatoes can in some ways be the most problematic. Fresh tomatoes available in many grocery stores simply lack flavor and may be under–ripe and "pappy". They may have been imported from large glasshouses, having been picked while still green. If you want to use fresh tomatoes, look for soft, juicy tomatoes that are really ripe. Vine-ripened tomatoes can be good, as are home grown tomatoes, in season.

The alternative is to use good canned tomatoes, and there are some excellent varieties available.

To counteract any sharpness, try adding half a teaspoon of sugar to the tomato mixture. Another good tip is to add a little milk to a tomato sauce—this gives a richness and smoothness which is quite unexpected.

Sun-dried tomatoes, and the more recently available sun-blush tomatoes, are also good to have in your store cupboard to add interest to any tomato-based recipe.

Cheese

Buy a lovely chunk of Parmigiano Reggiano (Parmesan) cheese and keep it in the refrigerator. Then, with some excellent egg-based pasta, a bottle of extra virgin olive oil from your cupboard and a few herbs you can make the most excellent of simple dishes, pasta gratinati. For any Italian pasta cookery, Parmesan cheese is a must—but do not buy the ready-grated cheese in a packet or jar—this is sometimes little better than sawdust. Choose freshly grated or shaved Parmesan every time!

Pecorino cheese is another hard Italian cheese much loved in this type of cooking. It is made from ewes' milk and can have an even stronger flavor than Parmesan. Either of these cheeses can be added to pasta sauces, sprinkled over the top of lasagne or cannelloni before baking, or simply grated over a finished dish. Mascarpone, ricotta and mozzarella are other Italian cheeses that frequently feature in pasta cooking. As with Parmesan, buy the best quality you can afford—the results will always reflect the price.

Other Store Cupboard Ingredients

Pesto

As well as having a selection of dried pasta to hand, make sure that you also have a jar or two of ready-made pesto sauce—these can be basil, red pepper or sun-dried tomato-based varieties. Then, a simple pasta meal is never far away!

Olives and Olive-based Tapenade

There are lots of different olives available in the shops. Choose some large black or green ones bottled in olive oil, or try wrinkly Greek-style black olives for an even stronger flavor. Green and black olive tapenades are sold in jars and can be stirred into cooked pasta to create an easy, quick meal, finished off with a few shavings of Parmesan cheese over the top. Remember to pit your olives if they are not already stoned.

Jars of Antipasto

Artichoke hearts, sun-dried tomatoes, cultivated mushrooms and wild mushrooms, and red peppers all come bottled in olive oil. Simply take one or other of these ingredients, drain and stir into cooked pasta with a little of the olive oil from the jar.

Dried Wild Mushrooms

Although these seem expensive, all you need is a few pieces soaked in hot water and added to a sauce to create a wonderful flavor—and of course they will keep for ages in an airtight container. Try adding a few rehydrated wild mushrooms to a dish of macaroni cheese before cooking... delicious!

Campanelle with Rabbit and Olive Sauce

Campanelle with Rabbit and Olive Sauce

Campanelle pasta, sometimes referred to as gigli or riccioli, is best served with a thick sauce and is perfectly suited to this rabbit and olive recipe.

You will need:
- 12 oz (350 g) rabbit meat (boned)
- juice of 1 lemon
- 1 tsp dried mixed herbs
- 2 tbsp olive oil
- 1 onion, finely chopped
- 2 cloves garlic, peeled and crushed
- 1 sprig fresh rosemary
- 1 sprig fresh thyme
- 3–4 leaves fresh sage, chopped small bunch fresh parsley, chopped
- 3 oz (75 g) black olives
- 14 oz (400 g) canned chopped tomatoes
- ½ tsp sugar
- 1 tsp Dijon mustard
- 12 oz (350 g) campanelle

Serves 4

1. Cut the boned rabbit meat into small chunks and put into a bowl. Add the lemon juice and mixed herbs and mix well. Cover and leave in a cool place for 1–2 hours to marinate.

2. Heat the oil in a large pan over a medium heat. Drain the rabbit meat, reserving the marinade and cook in the oil for five minutes, browning on all sides. Remove from the oil, and then cook the onion and garlic in the oil until soft. Return the rabbit to the pan, along with the herbs, olives, tomatoes, sugar, Dijon mustard and the reserved marinade. Bring to the boil, cover the pan and then lower the heat. Cook very gently for 40–45 minutes until the rabbit is tender.

3. Meanwhile, cook the campanelle in plenty of boiling, salted water until al dente and drain. Check the rabbit sauce and if it is very watery, increase the heat and reduce the sauce until it is thick.

Campanelle alla Carbonara

Campanelle alla Carbonara

The origins of this recipe are steeped in legend. Some believe it was created by the Carbonari, a secret society prominent in the unifications of Italy.

You will need:

- 2 tbsp olive oil
- 1 small onion, finely chopped
- 7 oz (200 g) streaky bacon or pancetta, cut into cubes
- 12 oz (350 g) campanelle
- 4 eggs
- 4 tbsp heavy cream
- 75 g (3 oz) freshly grated Parmesan cheese
- salt and black pepper

Serves 4

1. Heat the oil in a large pan over a medium heat. Add the onion and cook for 4–5 minutes until soft. Add the bacon or pancetta and carry on cooking for another 7–8 minutes, stirring all the time.

2. Meanwhile, cook the campanelle in plenty of boiling, salted water until al dente. Lightly whisk the eggs and cream together in a bowl. Add 2 oz (50 g) of the Parmesan cheese and season with a little salt and plenty of black pepper.

3. Drain the pasta and tip into the pan with the onion and bacon. Turn off the heat under the pan and add the egg and cream mixture. Toss everything together vigorously so that the egg cooks in the hot pasta. Serve with extra black pepper and the rest of the Parmesan cheese.

19

Cannelloni with Ricotta and Broccoli (v)

Cannelloni with Ricotta and Broccoli (v)

This classic pasta dish was invented in 1907 by the celebrated chef, Salvatore Coletta, in Sorrento, Italy.

You will need:

- 12 oz (350 g) broccoli florets
- 12 oz (350 g) ricotta cheese or drained cottage cheese
- 2 cloves garlic, peeled and crushed
- 1 tsp dried basil
- 4 oz (100 g) freshly grated Parmesan cheese
- salt and pepper
- 16 dried cannelloni tubes

For the tomato sauce:

- 1 tbsp olive oil
- 1 oz (25 g) butter
- 1 large onion, finely chopped
- 1 clove garlic, peeled and crushed
- 1 lb, 2 oz (560 g) jar passata (sieved tomatoes)
- 8 fl.oz (250 ml) water
- 1 tsp sugar
- ½ tsp dried oregano
- salt and black pepper
- 4 fl.oz (100 ml) milk

Serves 4

1. Begin by making the tomato sauce. Heat the oil and butter in a large pan over a medium heat. Add the onion and garlic and cook for ten minutes until golden and soft. Add the passata, water, sugar and oregano and bring to the boil. Lower the heat and slowly simmer for ten minutes. Season with salt and black pepper, add the milk and continue to simmer gently for another 10–15 minutes.

2. Steam the broccoli florets for 5–8 minutes until just soft. Set aside to cool.

3. Heat the oven to 375°F / 190°C. Put the ricotta, garlic, basil and 1 oz (25 g) of the Parmesan cheese into a bowl, and mix together well using a fork. Add the steamed broccoli and mix in. Season with salt and pepper. Add a little olive oil if the mixture seems very stiff.

4. Put a little of the tomato sauce in the bottom of a large shallow baking dish. Fill each of the cannelloni tubes with ricotta mixture and lay them side by side in the dish. Pour the rest of the tomato sauce over the cannelloni, then sprinkle with the remaining Parmesan cheese. Bake in the oven for 40 minutes until the top is brown and bubbling and the pasta is cooked.

Capellini with Crab, Peas and Mint

Capellini with Crab, Peas and Mint

Capellini is a long and narrow pasta that is best accompanied by light vegetables. This recipe is a perfect summer dish.

You will need:

- 1 lb (450 g) mixed white and brown crab meat
- juice of 2 lemons
- grated rind of 1 lemon
- 4–6 tbsp olive oil
- 1 small red onion, finely chopped
- 1 clove garlic, peeled and crushed
- 4 oz (100 g) fresh or frozen peas, cooked
- handful of fresh mint leaves, chopped or 1 tsp dried mint, grated
- salt and black pepper
- 12 oz (350 g) capellini

Serves 4

1. Put the crab meat into a bowl with the lemon juice and rind and mix well.

2. Heat the oil in a pan over a medium heat. Add the onion and garlic and cook for 5–10 minutes, taking care not to burn the mixture. Add the crab meat, peas and mint, season with salt and pepper and mix well.

3. Meanwhile, cook the capellini pasta in a large pan of boiling water until al dente. Drain, reserving 3–4 tablespoons of the cooking liquid. Add the cooked pasta to the crab mixture, together with the reserved liquid, and toss until well mixed. Drizzle a little extra olive oil and grind some more black pepper over each serving. Garnish with mint leaves.

Casarecce with Sausage and Black Olives

Casarecce with Sausage and Black Olives

Casarecce is a scroll-shaped pasta from southern Italy. The s-shape of the pasta means that it will retain the rich sauce of this recipe.

You will need:
- 1 tbsp olive oil
- 1 onion, finely chopped
- 12 oz (350 g) uncooked spicy sausages, cut into pieces 2 in. (2.5 cm) long
- 14 oz (400 g) canned chopped tomatoes
- 4 fl.oz (100 ml) dry white wine
- ½ tsp sugar
- a sprig of fresh rosemary
- 12 black olives, pitted
- 12 oz (350 g) casarecce
- salt and black pepper
- a handful of basil leaves
- Parmesan cheese shavings

Serves 4

1. Heat the oil in a pan over a medium heat. Add the onion and the pieces of sausage and cook gently, stirring from time to time, until the sausages begin to brown.

2. Drain the tomatoes, reserving the juice. Add the tomatoes to the sausages with the wine, sugar and rosemary. Continue to cook over a low heat for another 10–15 minutes. Add the olives during the last five minutes of cooking.

3. Meanwhile, cook the pasta in plenty of boiling, salted water until al dente. Drain, and reserve a few spoonfuls of the cooking liquid.

4. Add the cooking liquid to the sausage mixture. Season with salt and black pepper. Put the drained pasta into the pan of sauce with the torn basil leaves, toss well and serve with shavings of Parmesan cheese and drizzle over a little extra olive oil.

Rustic Chickpea and Pasta Soup

Rustic Chickpea and Pasta Soup

This is a fast, hearty meal that is perfect for the winter months. This dish can be served as a starter with a light main course to follow.

You will need:
- 1 tbsp olive oil
- 1 onion, finely chopped
- 2 cloves garlic, peeled and crushed
- 4 oz (100 g) pancetta or thin streaky bacon, cut into small strips
- 1 lb, 12 oz (800 g) canned chickpeas
- 4–5 large, juicy tomatoes, skinned and chopped
- 1 tsp dried mixed herbs
- 20 fl.oz (600 ml) vegetable or chicken stock
- 3 oz (75 g) small conchiglie
- 2 bay leaves
- salt and ground black pepper
- 2–3 tbsp fresh parsley, chopped

Serves 4

1. Heat the oil in a large pan over a medium heat. Add the onion and garlic and cook for five minutes until soft. Add the pancetta or bacon and cook for a further five minutes.

2. Drain the chickpeas and reserve 5 fl.oz (150 ml) of the liquid. Put half of the chickpeas in a bowl and mash with a fork. Add to the pan with the rest of the chickpeas, together with the tomatoes, mixed herbs, stock and reserved chickpea liquid. Add the conchiglie pasta and bay leaves, stirring to separate the pasta. Bring to the boil, lower the heat and cook for a further 10–15 minutes until the pasta is cooked. Remove the bay leaves, season with salt and pepper and serve sprinkled with parsley and drizzled with a little extra olive oil.

Conchiglie Stuffed with Crispy Duck

Conchiglie Stuffed with Crispy Duck

Conchiglie is one of the most popular pasta types in Britain.

You will need:
- 1 quantity of tomato sauce (see p. 21)
- 2 tsp sweet chili sauce
- 3–4 tbsp chopped flat-leaf parsley or coriander leaves
- 20 large conchiglie shells
- 3–4 cooked duck legs
- 2 tbsp olive oil
- 8 small scallions, cut into thin strips
- 1 red pepper, cut into thin strips
- 3–4 tbsp fresh breadcrumbs

Serves 4

1. Put the tomato sauce into a pan and simmer for ten minutes until thick. Add the sweet chili sauce and the parsley or coriander.

2. Cook the conchiglie in plenty of boiling, salted water until al dente. Drain and put into cold water until ready to use.

3. Strip the meat from the bones of the duck legs, cutting it into strips. Cut the skin up as well (if liked) as using this will make the duck very crispy. Heat the oil in a shallow pan over a medium heat and add the shredded duck meat and skin (if using). Cook for 5–6 minutes until the meat starts to brown.

4. Heat the oven to 375°F / 190°C. Put some of the tomato sauce in the base of a shallow dish. Remove the conchiglie, one at a time, and shake dry. Stuff each shell with duck meat, scallions and red pepper strips. Place the stuffed shells on top of the tomato sauce. Pour a little of the remaining sauce over each shell, sprinkle with breadcrumbs and a drizzle of olive oil. Bake in the oven for about 10–15 minutes, until the sauce is bubbling hot.

Conchiglie with Mussels and Saffron

Conchiglie with Mussels and Saffron

Conchiglie is the perfect pasta for this classic seafood recipe. Ideal when served with a glass of chilled white wine.

You will need:

- 2 lb (1 kg) mussels
- 4 fl.oz (100 ml) water
- 2 oz (50 g) butter
- 2–3 shallots, finely chopped
- 2 cloves garlic, peeled and crushed
- pinch saffron threads, soaked in a little boiling water
- 4 fl.oz (100 ml) white wine
- 4 fl.oz (100 ml) heavy cream
- 12 oz (350 g) small conchiglie
- salt and black pepper
- fresh parsley

Serves 4

1. Scrub and debeard the mussels, discarding any which have cracked shells or are not tightly closed. Put them and the water into a large pan over a medium heat. Cover the pan and steam the mussels, shaking occasionally until they open, for 4–5 minutes. Remove the mussels with a slotted spoon, discarding any that do not open. Pour off and reserve the clear cooking juices, discarding the sandy residue. Remove the mussels from their shells.

2. Melt the butter in a pan over a medium heat. Add the shallots and garlic and cook for 5–7 minutes. Add the saffron with the soaking water and the wine and cook for another 5 minutes. Stir in the cream, and cook for a further 2–3 minutes.

3. Meanwhile, cook the conchiglie pasta in plenty of boiling, salted water until al dente. Drain the pasta and add to the shallot mixture, together with the mussels and toss well, adding a little of the mussel liquid if necessary. Season with salt and black pepper, sprinkle with parsley and serve.

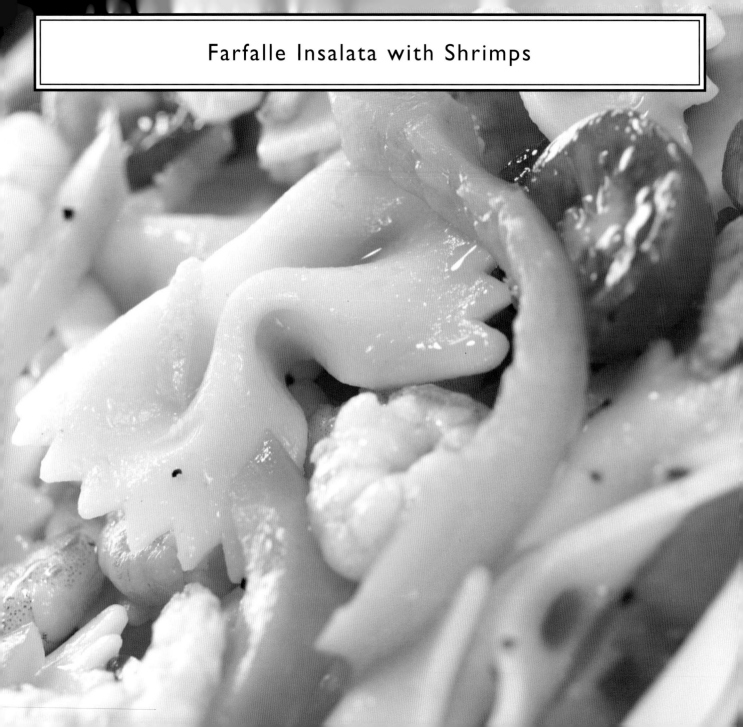

Farfalle Insalata with Shrimps

Farfalle Insalata with Shrimps

This colorful summer pasta salad combines shrimps, peppers and tomatoes to produce mouth-watering results.

You will need:
- 1 orange pepper
- 4 tbsp olive oil
- ½ small red chili
- 3 cloves garlic, peeled and finely sliced
- ½ tsp fennel seeds
- 1 lb (450 g) cooked shelled shrimps
- ½ tsp fish sauce or anchovy essence
- 12 oz (350 g) farfalle
- grated rind and juice of ½ small lemon
- 8 oz (225 g) cherry tomatoes, cut in half if large
- salt and black pepper
- small bunch of fresh fennel leaves, snipped

Serves 4

1. Put the pepper under a medium grill, turning until the skin is blackened all over. Put the pepper into a plastic bag until cool.

2. Put the olive oil into a shallow pan over a low heat. Add the chili, garlic and fennel seeds. Cook very gently for 4–5 minutes until the garlic is soft, taking care not to burn it. Add the shrimps and the fish sauce, and cook very gently for another 2–3 minutes.

3. Meanwhile, cook the farfalle in plenty of boiling, salted water until al dente. Drain, and then toss in the oil and shrimp mixture. Add the lemon rind and juice and set aside to cool.

4. Peel off the blackened skin of the pepper and cut into thin strips. Add the pepper strips and the cherry tomatoes to the cold pasta mixture. Season with salt and black pepper and serve sprinkled with the snipped fennel.

Farfalle with Ham, Rocket and Pine Nuts

Farfalle with Ham, Rocket and Pine Nuts

Ham, rocket and pine nuts make a winning combination in this timeless farfalle dish.

You will need:
- 12 oz (350 g) farfalle
- 4 oz (100 g) ricotta cheese
- 3 oz (75 g) grated pecorino cheese
- 2 oz (50 g) butter
- 4 slices of ham, cut into thin strips
- 2 handfuls of rocket leaves
- salt and black pepper
- 1 oz (25 g) toasted pine nuts

Serves 4

1. Cook the pasta in plenty of boiling, salted water until al dente. Drain, reserving a few spoonfuls of the cooking water. Put the pasta back into the pan with the ricotta, 2 oz (50 g) of the pecorino cheese and the butter. Stir over a low heat, adding a little of the cooking water if necessary, until well mixed together.

2. Add the ham and the rocket, stir well and season with salt and pepper. Serve sprinkled with the toasted pine nuts and the remainder of the pecorino cheese.

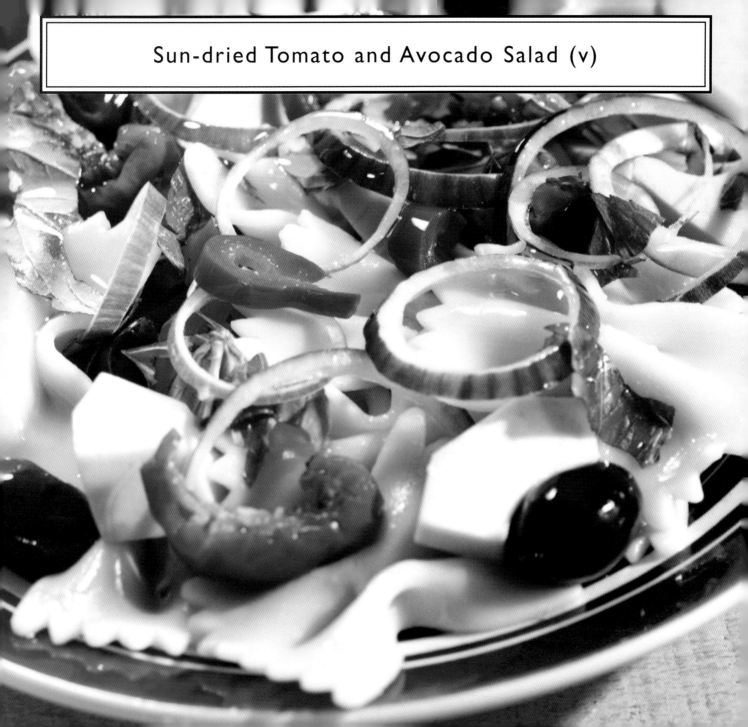

Sun-dried Tomato and Avocado Salad (v)

Sun-dried Tomato and Avocado Salad (v)

An easy-to-prepare pasta salad that packs a real punch in the flavor department.

You will need:

- 12 oz (350 g) farfalle
- 1 tbsp olive oil
- 12 sun-dried tomatoes in olive oil, cut in half if large
- 12 black olives, pitted and drained
- 2 cloves garlic, peeled and crushed
- 1 bottled or canned roasted red pepper, cut into thin strips
- 1 small red onion, cut into fine rings
- 1 large avocado
- juice of 1 lemon
- a handful of fresh mint leaves, roughly chopped
- salt and black pepper

Serves 4

1. Cook the pasta in plenty of boiling, salted water. Drain and put into a large bowl with the olive oil and toss well.

2. Add the sun-dried tomatoes in their olive oil, together with the olives, garlic, pepper strips and red onion. Set aside to cool.

3. Cut the avocado into quarters, removing the stone. Peel and cut into chunks. Coat the avocado flesh with the lemon juice. Add to the cold pasta with the mint leaves. Season with salt and pepper and toss gently together.

Fettuccine with Lobster and Cream

Fettuccine with Lobster and Cream

An extravagant pasta dish for special occasions. This dish originates from the beautiful region of Sicily.

You will need:

- meat from 1 cooked lobster
- juice of 1 lemon
- 2 oz (50 g) butter
- leaves from 2 or 3 sprigs of fresh marjoram
- 2 fl.oz (50 ml) heavy cream
- 4 fl.oz (100 ml) fruity white wine
- 1 tbsp fish sauce
- salt and black pepper
- 12 oz (350 g) fettuccine

Serves 4

1. Cut the lobster meat into small chunks and toss it in the lemon juice. Heat the butter gently in a pan over a low heat. Add the lobster and lemon juice together, with the marjoram, and cook gently for 2–3 minutes.

2. Add the cream, wine and fish sauce, stirring all the time. Season with salt and pepper and continue to cook for another 2–3 minutes. Remove from the heat.

3. Cook the fettuccine in plenty of boiling, salted water until al dente. Drain, reserving a few spoonfuls of the cooking liquid. Tip the pasta into the lobster sauce, and mix together gently over a low heat, adding a little of the pasta cooking liquid if necessary. Serve with extra salt and some black pepper.

Fettuccine Arrabiata (v)

Fettuccine Arrabiata (v)

Cook up a healthy taste sensation for your family in under half an hour—simply delicious!

You will need:
- 2 tbsp olive oil
- 1 onion, finely chopped
- 2 cloves garlic, peeled and crushed
- 1 small red chili, deseeded and finely chopped
- 1 lb, 12 oz (800 g) canned chopped tomatoes
- ½ tsp sugar
- salt and black pepper
- 12 oz (350 g) fettuccine
- 2 tbsp freshly chopped parsley

Serves 4

1. Heat the oil in a pan over a medium heat. Add the onion, garlic and chili and cook gently for 5–6 minutes until soft, taking care not to burn them. Add the tomatoes and sugar and season with salt and pepper. Continue to cook for another 10–15 minutes. Remove from the heat and liquidize the sauce in a blender or food processor.

2. Meanwhile, cook the fettuccine in plenty of boiling, salted water until al dente. Drain the pasta, reserving a few spoonfuls of the cooking liquid. Toss the pasta in the sauce, adding a little of the cooking liquid if necessary. Serve, drizzled with a little extra olive oil and sprinkled with chopped parsley.

Sicilian Fusilli

Sicilian Fusilli

This fantastic fusilli recipe is the godfather of all pasta dishes! Top quality steak will greatly improve the recipe.

You will need:
- 2 tbsp olive oil
- 1 onion, finely chopped
- 2 cloves garlic, peeled and crushed
- 1 stick of celery
- 12 oz (350 g) sirloin steak, cut into thin strips
- 2 oz (50 g) pine nuts
- 2 oz (50 g) sultanas
- 14 oz (400 g) canned chopped tomatoes
- 6 fl.oz (150 ml) passata
- 4–5 tbsp red wine
- 1 tsp dried mixed herbs
- salt and black pepper
- 12 oz (350 g) fusilli
- a few sprigs of fresh parsley

Serves 4

1. Heat the oil in a large, shallow pan over a medium heat. Add the onion, garlic, celery and sirloin steak and cook, stirring occasionally, for 8–10 minutes, until the vegetables are soft and the beef is cooked.

2. Add the pine nuts, sultanas, tomatoes, passata, red wine and mixed herbs, mixing well. Cook for another 10–15 minutes, adding a little water if the sauce seems too thick. Season with salt and pepper.

3. Meanwhile, cook the fusilli in plenty of boiling, salted water until al dente. Drain the pasta and add to the sauce in the pan. Serve, sprinkled with sprigs of parsley.

Baked Piedmontese Fusilli with Sage and Anchovies

Baked Piedmontese Fusilli with Sage and Anchovies

The spiral shapes of this pasta perfectly catch the flavors of the anchovies during cooking.

You will need:
- 12 oz (350 g) fusilli
- 3 oz (75 g) butter
- 4 oz (100 g) mozzarella cheese, finely chopped
- 3 oz (75 g) freshly grated Parmesan cheese
- 10 leaves fresh sage, roughly chopped
- 4 canned anchovies, drained and cut into thin strips
- salt and black pepper

Serves 4

1. Heat the oven to 400°F / 200°C. Cook the fusilli in plenty of boiling, salted water until al dente. Drain, reserving a few spoonfuls of the cooking liquid.

2. Return the pasta to the pan with the butter, and stir over a low heat until the butter has melted. Add the mozzarella cheese, 2 oz (50 g) of the Parmesan cheese, the sage and anchovy strips along with a little of the cooking liquid if necessary. Season with salt and black pepper.

3. Put the pasta mixture into a shallow buttered ovenproof dish. Sprinkle with the rest of the Parmesan cheese and cook in the oven for 10–15 minutes, until golden brown and crunchy on top.

Note: *Omit the anchovies for a vegetarian dish.*

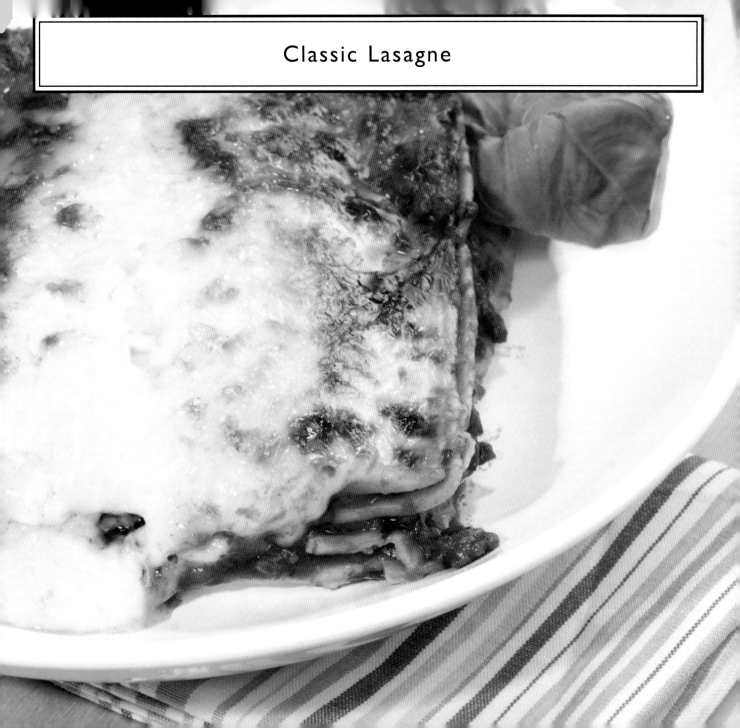

Classic Lasagne

Classic Lasagne

Lasagne is a firm favorite pasta dish around the world!

You will need:
- 12 dried lasagne sheets
- 1 tbsp olive oil
- 1 oz (25 g) butter
- 6 oz (150 g) button mushrooms (or your favorite variety)
- 1 quantity of Bolognese sauce (see p. 83)
- 2 oz (50 g) freshly grated Parmesan cheese

For the white sauce:
- 2 oz (50 g) butter
- 1 oz (25 g) plain flour
- 10 fl.oz (300 ml) milk
- 2 oz (50 g) cheddar cheese, grated

Serves 4

1. Heat the oven to 375°F / 190°C. Heat the olive oil and butter in a large pan over a medium heat. Add the mushrooms and cook gently until soft. Add the Bolognese sauce and mix well. Remove from the heat.

2. Heat the butter in a saucepan until it has melted. Add the flour and stir, then pour in the milk, stirring until the sauce thickens and is a smooth consistency. Add the cheese and stir to combine.

3. Put about one third of the meat sauce into the base of a square or oblong baking dish; cover with about one third of the white sauce and about one third of the lasagne sheets. Repeat the layers, finishing with a layer of lasagne topped with white sauce. Sprinkle with the Parmesan cheese and bake in the oven for 25–30 minutes, until bubbling and brown on top.

Cod and Broccoli Lasagne

Cod and Broccoli Lasagne

A flavorsome variation on the usual meat lasagne. Perfect for warm, summer evenings with family or friends.

You will need:
- 12 dried lasagne sheets
- 12 oz (350 g) cod fillet, skinned and cut into pieces
- 6 fl.oz (150 ml) milk
- 8 oz (225 g) broccoli florets
- 1 tbsp olive oil
- 1 onion, finely chopped
- 4 oz (100 g) cherry tomatoes
- 2 tbsp chopped fresh parsley
- 1 quantity of white sauce (see p. 47)
- 4 oz (100 g) cheddar cheese, grated

Serves 4

1. Heat the oven to 375°F / 190°C. Put the cod into a shallow pan, cover with the milk and cook gently over a low heat until the cod is just cooked and opaque. Drain the fish, put on to a plate and flake with a fork.

2. Steam the broccoli florets until just cooked. Heat the oil in a pan over a medium heat, add the onion and cook for 5–7 minutes until golden. Remove from the heat. Add the cod and broccoli to the pan, together with the cherry tomatoes, and mix well.

3. Brush the inside of a square baking dish with some olive oil. Mix the parsley into the white sauce and put a thin layer of the sauce in the bottom of the dish. Cover with about one third of the cod and broccoli mixture and sprinkle with one third of the cheese and one third of the lasagne sheets. Repeat the layers, finishing with a layer of lasagne, topped with white sauce and the remaining cheese. Bake for 30–35 minutes until bubbling and brown on top.

Griddled Scallops, Bacon and Chili

Griddled Scallops, Bacon and Chili

This recipe is a sophisticated and appetizing starter that is bound to impress your dinner guests.

You will need:
- 12 oz (350 g) linguine
- 3 tbsp olive oil
- ½ small red chili, deseeded and finely chopped
- 6 rashers of thinly sliced unsmoked streaky bacon, cut in small strips
- 8 oz (225 g) cherry tomatoes
- 12 oz (350 g) scallops, cut in half
- salt and black pepper

Serves 4

1. Cook the linguine in plenty of boiling, salted water until al dente.

2. Meanwhile, put the oil into a large griddle pan over a medium heat. Add the chili and bacon and cook for 3–4 minutes until the bacon starts to brown. Add the cherry tomatoes and the scallops and cook for 2–3 minutes, until the scallops are opaque and the tomatoes begin to go soft. Season with salt and pepper.

3. Drain the pasta, toss in a little extra olive oil and then add the sauce, tossing to coat.

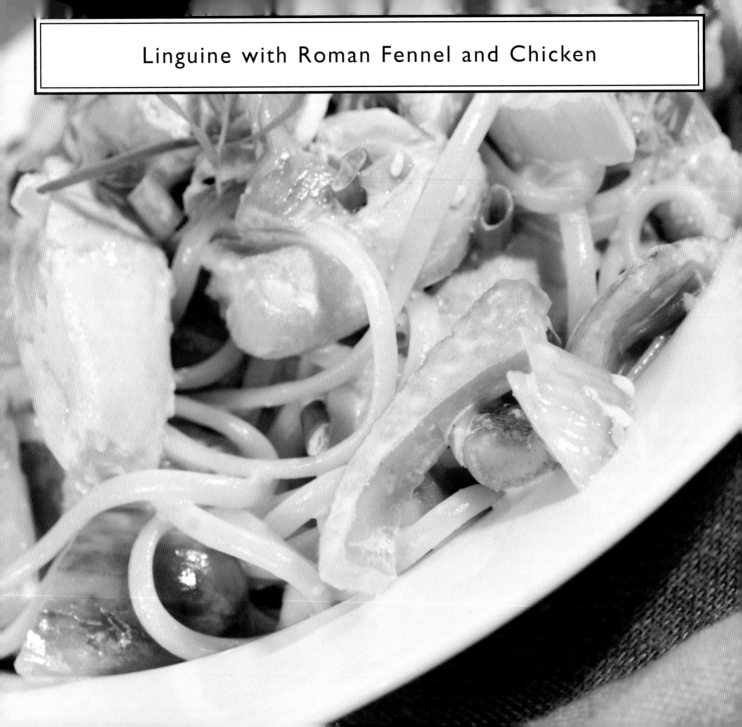

Linguine with Roman Fennel and Chicken

Linguine with Roman Fennel and Chicken

The sauce leads the way in this delicious and satisfying linguine recipe.

You will need:

- 1 tbsp olive oil
- 12 oz (350 g) skinless chicken breasts, cut into chunks
- 2 oz (50 g) butter
- 6 scallions, finely sliced
- 1 clove garlic, peeled and crushed
- 1 head fennel, cut into small pieces
- juice of ½ lemon
- 4 tbsp crème fraîche
- 2–3 tbsp chicken stock
- salt and black pepper
- 12 oz (350 g) linguine
- 2 tbsp chopped fresh tarragon

Serves 4

1. Heat the oil in a frying pan over a medium heat. Add the chicken breast pieces, a few at a time, and brown on all sides. Remove and set aside while cooking the rest.

2. Melt the butter in a large pan over a medium heat. Add the scallions and garlic and cook for 4–5 minutes until soft. Add the fennel and carry on cooking for another 2–3 minutes. Add the chicken into the pan.

3. Stir in the lemon juice, crème fraîche and two tablespoons of the chicken stock. Cook gently for another 5–7 minutes until the chicken is cooked through. Add a little extra chicken stock if necessary. Season with salt and pepper.

4. Meanwhile, cook the linguine in plenty of boiling, salted water until al dente; drain and toss with the sauce, coating well. Serve sprinkled with the tarragon.

Wholewheat Macaroni Cheese (v)

Wholewheat Macaroni Cheese (v)

This is a healthy, wholewheat pasta dish that is ideal for children.

You will need:
- 2 oz (50 g) butter
- 1 onion, finely chopped
- 6 oz (150 g) button mushrooms, cut in quarters (or your favorite variety)
- 2 oz (50 g) fine wholewheat flour
- 1 tsp Dijon mustard
- 30 fl.oz (900 ml) milk
- 4 oz (100 g) grated cheddar cheese
- salt and pepper
- 12 oz (350 g) wholewheat, short-cut macaroni
- 1 oz (25 g) freshly grated Parmesan cheese
- 2 tbsp fresh breadcrumbs

Serves 4

1. Heat the oven to 375°F / 190°C. Melt the butter in a pan over a medium heat. Add the onion and mushrooms and cook for 5–6 minutes until soft. Sprinkle over the flour, and using a wooden spoon, mix over the heat for 1–2 minutes. Remove from the heat.

2. Add the Dijon mustard and then the milk, a little at a time, mixing well between additions. When all of the milk is incorporated, return the pan to the heat and bring to a gentle simmer, stirring all the time. Cook until the sauce is thick and creamy. Mix in the cheddar cheese, season with salt and pepper, and remove from the heat.

3. Cook the macaroni in plenty of boiling, salted water. Drain and add to the cheese sauce. Pour the macaroni and sauce into an ovenproof dish, and sprinkle with the Parmesan cheese and breadcrumbs. Bake in the oven for 15–20 minutes until golden brown and bubbling.

Baked Macaroni Pie

Baked Macaroni Pie

This delicious pie alternative to regular macaroni cheese is destined to become a frequent addition to the dinner time menu.

You will need:
- 10 oz (300 g) short-cut macaroni
- 1 tbsp olive oil
- 4 oz (100 g) small mushrooms, finely sliced
- 1 quantity of Bolognese sauce (see p. 83)
- 1 lb (450 g) spinach
- 1 oz (25 g) butter
- salt and black pepper
- 3 oz (75 g) freshly grated Parmesan cheese
- 1 quantity of white sauce (see p. 47)

Serves 4

1. Heat the oven to 375°F / 190°C. Cook the macaroni in plenty of boiling, salted water. Drain and set aside.

2. Heat the oil in a pan over a medium heat and cook the mushrooms until soft. Mix the mushrooms into the Bolognese sauce.

3. Wash the spinach well. Melt the butter in a large pan over a low heat. Add the spinach, pressing down well. Cover the pan and cook the spinach for 5–7 minutes, shaking the pan from time to time, until the spinach is cooked. Chop the cooked spinach finely and season with salt and pepper.

4. Stir 2 oz (50 g) of the Parmesan cheese into the white sauce. Brush the inside of a deep ovenproof dish with olive oil. Put half of the sauce on the bottom of the dish. Cover with half of the spinach and half of the macaroni. Repeat the layers, and then pour over the white sauce. Sprinkle with the rest of the Parmesan cheese. Bake in the oven for 35–45 minutes until bubbling and brown on top.

Mafalda with Green Olive Tapendale
& Vegetable Ribbons (v)

Mafalda with Green Olive Tapendale & Vegetable Ribbons (v)

Pasta is a truly versatile cooking ingredient for vegetarian recipes. This authentic Italian dish dispels the myth that vegetarian cuisine is bland.

You will need:

- 12 oz (350 g) mafalda
- 2 small zucchini
- 2 long, thin carrots
- 1 long, thin red pepper
- 2 tbsp olive oil
- 2 tbsp green olive tapenade
- 10–12 green olives, pitted

Serves 4

1. Cook the mafalda pasta in plenty of boiling, salted water until al dente.

2. Meanwhile, cut the zucchini and carrots into thin ribbons using a vegetable peeler. Cut the pepper into long, thin strips. Heat the olive oil in a shallow pan over a low heat. Cook the pieces of zucchini, carrot and pepper for 3–4 minutes until just beginning to brown.

3. Drain the pasta and put into a warmed serving bowl. Stir in the green olive tapenade, add the olives and the vegetable pieces in olive oil and toss gently together.

Mafalda with Ricotta, Broad Beans & Crispy Pancetta

Mafalda with Ricotta, Broad Beans & Crispy Pancetta

This delicious dish, with an unusual type of pasta, is sure to appeal to the more sophisticated dinner guest!

You will need:
- 4 oz (100 g) fresh or frozen broad beans, shelled weight
- 4–6 rashers of pancetta or thinly cut smoked streaky bacon
- 4 oz (100 g) ricotta cheese
- 2 tbsp light cream
- 2 tbsp fresh chopped mint
- 12 oz (350 g) mafalda
- 1 tbsp olive oil
- salt and black pepper

Serves 4

1. Cook the broad beans in a pan of boiling, salted water until cooked—the time depends on the size and age of the broad beans. Drain, rinse in cold water and then slip the bright green beans out of their white skins. Set aside the beans and discard the skins.

2. Cook the pancetta or streaky bacon under a medium grill until crisp and brown. Set aside to cool. Mix the ricotta with the cream until smooth. Add the fresh chopped mint.

3. Cook the mafalda pasta in plenty of boiling, salted water until al dente. Drain the pasta and put into a warm serving bowl. Toss the pasta with the olive oil and then add the ricotta and mint mixture, incorporating together well. Add the broad beans and season with salt and black pepper. Break up the pieces of crispy pancetta or bacon and sprinkle them over the pasta.

Salad of Antipasto

Salad of Antipasto

With a variety of colors and flavors, this mouth-watering dish will become a favorite in no time.

You will need:
- 12 oz (350 g) malloreddus
- 4 artichoke hearts in olive oil
- 6 halves of sun-dried tomato in olive oil
- 6 very thin slices of Italian salami

Serves 4

1. Cook the pasta in plenty of boiling, salted water until al dente. Drain, rinse in cold water and drain well. Put the pasta into a shallow serving dish.

2. Cut each artichoke heart into four and each piece of sun-dried tomato into two. Cut the salami into thin strips. Toss the pasta with two tablespoons of the olive oil from the artichoke hearts and the tomatoes. Add the artichoke, sun-dried tomatoes and salami to the pasta and serve.

Tuna al Forno

Tuna al Forno

This is a soothing, comforting plateful to drive out the chill of the coldest winter evening. The tuna combined with the classic Italian ingredients deliver a match made in heaven for your taste buds.

You will need:
- 12 oz (350 g) orecchiete
- 2 tbsp olive oil
- 1 onion, finely chopped
- 2 cloves garlic, peeled and crushed
- 7 oz (200 g) canned tuna in olive oil, drained
- 4 canned anchovies in olive oil, drained and chopped
- 2 tbsp capers
- 14 oz (400 g) canned chopped tomatoes
- 2 oz (50 g) black olives, roughly chopped
- 5–6 fresh basil leaves, torn into shreds
- salt and black pepper
- 4 oz (100 g) mozzarella cheese, sliced
- 1 oz (25 g) shaved Parmesan

Serves 4

1. Heat the oven to 375°F / 190°C. Cook the orecchiete in plenty of boiling, salted water until almost al dente. Drain and reserve a few spoonfuls of the cooking liquid.

2. Heat the oil in a large pan over a medium heat. Add the onion and garlic and cook for 5–7 minutes until soft. Add the tuna, breaking up into chunks with a fork, anchovies, capers, tomatoes, olives and basil. Season with salt and pepper and stir over the heat for 1–2 minutes. Remove from the heat.

3. Brush the inside of a deep ovenproof dish with olive oil. Add the pasta to the sauce with the mozzarella cheese, together with a little of the cooking liquid if necessary. Mix well and put into the prepared dish. Sprinkle with the Parmesan cheese and bake in the oven for 15–20 minutes until brown and bubbling.

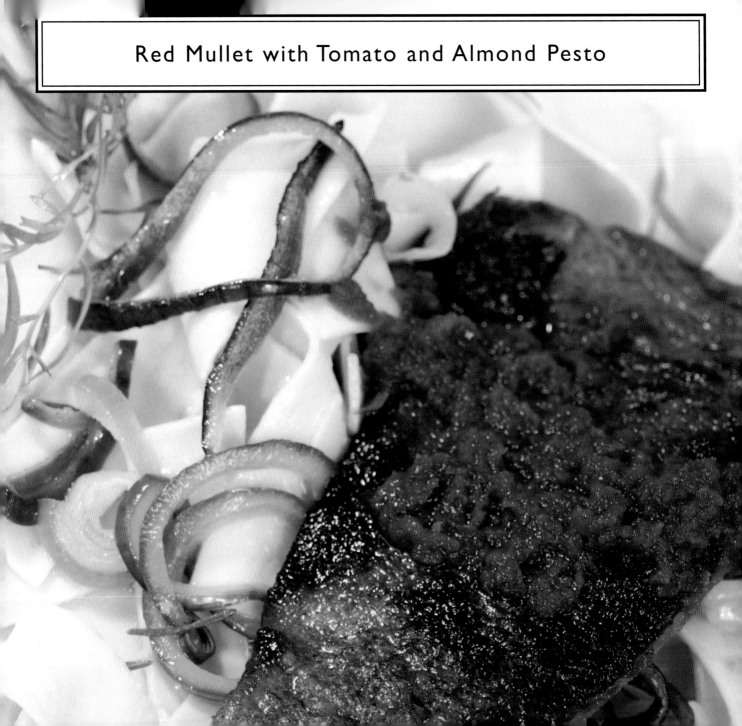

Red Mullet with Tomato and Almond Pesto

Red Mullet with Tomato and Almond Pesto

The rich flavor of the red mullet, combined with the lively pesto sauce and subtle flavor of the pasta makes this a great dish for family and friends.

You will need:
- 12 oz (350 g) pappardelle
- 4 fillets of red mullet

For the pesto:
- 2 oz (50 g) sun-dried tomatoes in olive oil
- 2 cloves garlic, peeled and crushed
- 2 oz (50 g) blanched almonds
- 1 oz (25 g) pecorino or Parmesan cheese, cut into small pieces
- 5 fl.oz (150 ml) olive oil
- 1 tsp red wine vinegar
- freshly ground black pepper

For the sauce:
- 1 oz (25 g) butter
- 1 red onion, finely sliced
- 3 fl.oz (75 ml) heavy cream or crème fraîche
- grated rind and juice of 1 lime
- 2 tbsp fresh tarragon leaves, roughly chopped

Serves 4

1. Make the pesto by putting all of the ingredients into a food processor or liquidizer and blending until smooth.

2. For the sauce, melt the butter in a pan over a medium heat. Add the onion and cook gently for 4–5 minutes until soft. Remove from the heat and stir in the cream, grated lime rind and tarragon.

3. Meanwhile, cook the pappardelle and cook the red mullet fillets on a hot griddle pan, two at a time, for 2–3 minutes on both sides until cooked through. Sprinkle each fillet with a little lime juice while cooking.

4. Drain the pasta and mix with the onion and cream mixture. Serve the pasta on four plates and top with a fillet of red mullet on each and 1–2 tablespoons of the pesto.

Penne Baked with Porcini, Cheese and Prosciutto

Penne Baked with Porcini, Cheese and Prosciutto

Whip up this tasty bake for a quick and satisfying meal—perfect for a cozy night in.

You will need:
- 12 oz (350 g) penne
- 2 oz (50 g) butter
- 1 stick celery, finely chopped
- 1 small onion, finely chopped
- 6 oz (150 g) mountain gorgonzola cheese, cut into cubes
- 4 fl.oz (100 ml) light cream
- 1 oz (15 g) dried porcini, soaked in hot water for 30 minutes
- 6–8 slices of prosciutto
- 2–3 tbsp fresh breadcrumbs

Serves 4

1. Heat the oven to 375°F / 190°C. Cook the penne in plenty of boiling, salted water until almost al dente.

2. Melt the butter in a pan over a medium heat. Add the celery and onion and cook for 7–8 minutes until soft. Add the cheese and 3 fl.oz (75 ml) of the cream. Stir over a low heat until the cheese has melted.

3. Drain the porcini and add to the cheese sauce. Cut the prosciutto into thin strips 2 in. (5 cm) long and stir into the sauce. Add the pasta to the sauce, mixing well. Add the remaining cream if necessary. Put into an oiled, shallow, ovenproof dish, sprinkle with the breadcrumbs and bake in the oven for 15–20 minutes until brown and bubbling.

Penne con Salsa di Noci (v)

Penne con Salsa di Noci (v)

The dash of chili powder brings an extra tang to this great dish. Add an extra pinch if you're feeling adventurous!

You will need:
- 4 oz (100 g) very fresh walnut pieces
- 3–4 cloves garlic, peeled and chopped
- 3 oz (75 g) freshly grated Parmesan cheese
- a pinch of mild chili powder
- 3 tbsp chopped fresh parsley
- 2 tbsp tomato paste
- 6 fl.oz (150 ml) olive oil
- 12 oz (350 g) penne

Serves 4

1. Put the walnuts, garlic, Parmesan cheese, chili powder, two tablespoons of the parsley and the tomato paste into the bowl of a liquidizer or food processor. Add 2 fl.oz (50 ml) of the olive oil and blend quickly. Continue adding the rest of the olive oil in small amounts, blending each addition until a loose consistency is reached.

2. Cook the penne in plenty of boiling, salted water until al dente. Drain, reserving a few spoonfuls of the cooking liquid. Toss the pasta in the walnut sauce, adding a little of the cooking liquid if necessary. Serve drizzled with a little extra olive oil and the rest of the parsley.

71

Radiatore with Mountain Gorgonzola (v)

Radiatore with Mountain Gorgonzola (v)

Said to resemble radiators, radiatore pasta works well with thicker sauces. This gorgeous gorgonzola sauce is the perfect accompaniment.

You will need:
- 2 oz (50 g) butter
- I stick celery, finely chopped
- I small onion, finely chopped
- 6 oz (150 g) mountain gorgonzola cheese, cut into cubes
- 4 fl.oz (100 ml) light cream
- 12 oz (350 g) radiatore
- a handful of fresh sage leaves, roughly chopped
- black pepper

Serves 4

1. Melt the butter in a pan over a medium heat. Add the celery and onion and cook for 7–8 minutes until soft. Add the cheese and 3 fl.oz (75 ml) of the cream. Stir over a low heat until the cheese has melted.

2. Cook the radiatore in plenty of boiling, salted water until al dente. Drain the pasta and add to the cheese sauce. Add the sage leaves, season with black pepper and stir gently over a low heat until well mixed, adding the remaining cream if necessary. Serve garnished with a little extra sage.

Ravioli Stuffed with Crab

Ravioli Stuffed with Crab

The oldest known recipe for ravioli dates back to an Anglo-Norman manuscript from the 1290s.

You will need:
- 1 quantity of fresh pasta made with 8 oz (225 g) flour (see p. 11)

For the filling:
- 6 oz (175 g) cream cheese
- 6 oz (175 g) brown and white crab meat
- 2 tbsp chopped fresh mint
- finely grated rind of 1 lime
- salt and black pepper

To finish:
- 3 oz (75 g) butter
- a small piece of red chili, deseeded and very finely chopped
- juice of 1 lime
- 2 tbsp chopped fresh parsley

Serves 4

1. Wrap the pasta dough in plastic wrap and leave to rest for 30 minutes.

2. Put all of the ingredients for the filling into a bowl and, using a wooden spoon, mix well together.

3. Cut the dough into four, and using a pasta machine, roll out a piece at a time into a long, thin sheet. Prepare all of the sheets and cover with plastic wrap to stop them drying out. Place one sheet on a floured board and put teaspoonfuls of the filling on the sheet in lines 2 in. (5 cm) apart. Cover with a second sheet of pasta and press down with your fingers to seal between the little heaps of filling. Using a fluted pastry wheel or sharp knife, cut between the filling, or use a 3 in. (7.5 cm) fluted or plain ravioli cutter. Repeat using the rest of the dough and filling. Set the ravioli aside in the refrigerator loosely covered until ready to cook.

4. Cook the ravioli, a few at a time, for about 3 minutes in plenty of boiling, salted water. Drain and put into a warmed serving dish. Melt the butter over a low heat with the chili, stir in the lime juice and pour over the ravioli. Toss together very gently and serve with the parsley.

Porcini Ravioli with Pesto Cream (v)

Porcini Ravioli with Pesto Cream (v)

The earthy and nutty flavor of porcini works perfectly alongside the pesto cream. "Porcini" means "piglets" in Italian, after the shape the mushrooms resemble.

You will need:
- 1 quantity of fresh pasta made with 8 oz (225 g) flour (see p. 11)

For the filling:
- 1 oz (25 g) dried porcini mushrooms
- 1 tbsp olive oil
- 1 small onion, finely chopped
- 3 oz (75 g) button mushrooms, very finely chopped
- 2 oz (50 g) ricotta cheese
- 3 oz (75 g) freshly grated Parmesan cheese
- salt and black pepper

For the sauce:
- 1 oz (25 g) butter
- 2 tbsp pesto sauce (see p. 89) or ready-made
- 2–3 tbsp light cream

Serves 4

1. Wrap the pasta dough in plastic wrap and leave to rest for 30 minutes.

2. Put the porcini into a bowl and cover with 5 fl.oz (150 ml) of boiling water. Leave to soak for 20–30 minutes. Drain, reserve the liquid and chop the porcini very finely. Heat the olive oil in a pan over a low heat. Add the onion, button mushrooms and porcini. Cook for about 5 minutes, then set aside to cool. Put the ricotta into a bowl, add the cooled mushroom mixture and 2 oz (50 g) of the Parmesan cheese. Season with salt and black pepper and mix well using a wooden spoon.

3. Cut the dough into four, and using a pasta machine, roll out a piece at a time into a long thin sheet. Prepare all of the sheets and cover with plastic wrap to stop them drying out. Place one sheet on a floured board and put teaspoonfuls of the filling on the sheet in lines 2 in. (5 cm) apart. Cover with a second sheet of pasta and press down with your fingers to seal between the little heaps of filling. Using a fluted pastry wheel or sharp knife, cut between the filling, or use a 3 in. (7.5 cm) fluted or plain ravioli cutter. Repeat using the rest of the dough and filling. Set the ravioli aside in the refrigerator loosely covered until ready to cook.

4. Cook the ravioli, a few at a time, for about 3 minutes in plenty of boiling, salted water. Drain and put into a warmed serving dish. Heat the butter and pesto in a pan over a low heat. Stir in the cream and pour over the ravioli. Toss together very gently and serve with the remaining Parmesan cheese.

Sicilian Rigatoni with Lamb

Sicilian Rigatoni with Lamb

The succulent lamb, alongside the sweet Sicilian flavors, guarantee a fantastic meal that you'll want to try again and again. Surveys show that rigatoni is the most popular pasta in Italy.

You will need:

- 2 lb, 3 oz (1 kg) leg of lamb
- 5–6 cloves garlic, peeled and sliced finely
- 3–4 sprigs fresh rosemary
- salt and pepper
- 4–5 tbsp olive oil
- 1 small red onion, sliced
- 1 red pepper, finely sliced
- 1 lb (450 g) sweet, juicy tomatoes, peeled and chopped
- 12 oz (350 g) rigatoni
- 2 oz (50 g) freshly grated pecorino cheese

Serves 4

1. Heat the oven to 325°F / 170°C.
   Use a sharp knife to make small incisions over the surface of the leg of lamb. Insert slivers of garlic and small sprigs of rosemary into the incisions. Rub in some salt and pepper.

2. Heat the oil in a roasting tray over a medium heat. Add the leg of lamb and brown all over. Remove from the heat and surround with the onion, red pepper and tomatoes. Cover with tin foil and roast in the oven for about two hours. Check after about 90 minutes and add a little water if the sauce is dry.

3. Remove the lamb from the oven and place on a warm serving dish, reserving the tomato mixture. Keep the lamb in a warm place while cooking the rigatoni in plenty of boiling, salted water until al dente. Drain the pasta, reserving a few spoonfuls of the cooking liquid. Put the pasta into a warm serving bowl, add the tomato mixture and toss together with a little of the pasta cooking liquid if necessary.

4. Cut slices of the lamb and serve with the pasta. To finish, sprinkle with the cheese.

Spaghetti alla Puttanesca

This spaghetti dish is fairly modern, with its earliest reference found in a 1960's novel. It is regarded, historically, as a dish that can be "thrown together" using store cupboard ingredients.

You will need:

- 4 tbsp olive oil
- 1 small onion, very finely chopped
- 3 cloves garlic, peeled and crushed
- 4 canned or bottled anchovies, drained and chopped
- 4 oz (100 g) black olives, roughly chopped
- 1 tbsp capers, drained
- 14 oz (400 g) canned tomatoes
- 2 tbsp flat-leaf parsley, chopped
- salt and black pepper
- 12 oz (350 g) spaghetti

Serves 4

1. Heat the oil in a pan over a low heat. Add the onion, garlic and anchovies and cook, stirring all the time, until the anchovies disintegrate. Add the olives and capers and cook for another minute or two.

2. Add the tomatoes and their juice together with one tablespoon of the parsley. Season with salt and pepper, bring to the boil, then cover the pan and cook very gently over a low heat for 20–25 minutes, stirring from time to time. Add a little extra water if necessary.

3. Meanwhile, cook the spaghetti in plenty of boiling, salted water until al dente. Drain and add to the hot sauce, tossing well. Serve sprinkled with the remaining parsley.

Classic Spaghetti Bolognese

Classic Spaghetti Bolognese

A classic dish that should grace the table of every household! Easy to make, this authentic spaghetti bolognese is perfect for cold, winter nights, accompanied by a glass of good red wine.

You will need:
- 2 oz (50 g) butter
- 2 tbsp olive oil
- 2 oz (50 g) pancetta or unsmoked streaky bacon, finely chopped
- 1 small onion, finely chopped
- 1 small carrot, finely chopped
- 1 stalk celery, finely chopped
- 2 cloves garlic, peeled and crushed
- 1 lb (450 g) lean beef steak mince
- 2 tbsp tomato paste
- 5 fl.oz (125 ml) white wine
- 5 fl.oz (125 ml) beef stock
- 3 fl.oz (75 ml) light cream
- salt and black pepper
- 12 oz (350 g) spaghetti
- 2 oz (50 g) freshly Parmesan cheese

Serves 4

1. Heat the butter and olive oil in a large pan over a medium heat. Add the pancetta or bacon, onion, carrot, celery and garlic and cook, stirring all the time, for 10 minutes until the vegetables are soft and golden.

2. Add the minced beef, tomato paste and wine and cook gently for another 10 minutes, stirring from time to time. Add the stock, cover the pan and cook very gently for 1–1½ hours, stirring from time to time, and adding a little extra wine, stock or water if the sauce becomes too dry. At the end of this cooking time, add the cream, season with salt and pepper, stir in and remove from the heat.

3. Cook the spaghetti in plenty of boiling, salted water until al dente. Drain the pasta and toss in the hot sauce. Serve sprinkled with the grated Parmesan cheese.

Spaghetti alle Vongole

Spaghetti alle Vongole

In Italy, this recipe varies from region to region and even between restaurants. The fresh clams give this dish a delightful, delicate taste.

You will need:

- 2 lb, 3 oz (1 kg) clams
- 5 fl.oz (125 ml) dry white wine
- 12 oz (350 g) spaghetti
- 4 tbsp olive oil
- 2 cloves garlic, peeled and finely sliced
- 3 tbsp flat-leaf parsley, chopped
- salt and black pepper

Serves 4

1. Scrub the clams under running water, discarding any which are open. Put them in a large pan with the wine and cook over a medium heat for about 5 minutes, shaking the pan frequently until the clams have opened.

2. Using a slotted spoon, transfer the clams to a bowl, discarding any which have not opened. Strain the liquid through a fine nylon sieve and set aside. Remove the clams from their shells, leaving a few intact for garnishing.

3. Cook the spaghetti in plenty of boiling water until al dente. Meanwhile, put the oil into a large pan over a low heat. Add the garlic and the shelled clams and cook for 2–3 minutes. Stir in the parsley and the strained liquid. Season with salt and pepper and cook for a further 2–3 minutes to reduce the liquid. Drain the spaghetti and toss in the clam sauce. Serve garnished with the clams in their shells.

Note: *You can also use drained, canned clams, adding them with the wine in step 3.*

Tagliatelle with Meatballs

Tagliatelle with Meatballs

In Italy, meatballs are known as "polpette" and are generally served as a second course. This meatball dish is rich and satisfying in flavor.

You will need:
- 1 quantity of tomato sauce (see p. 21)
- 12 oz (350 g) tagliatelle
- 2 tbsp fresh parsley

For the meatballs:
- 8 oz (225 g) minced pork
- 8 oz (225 g) minced beef
- 1 egg, beaten
- 2 oz (50 g) finely grated Parmesan cheese
- 2 cloves garlic, peeled and crushed
- 1 tsp dried oregano
- 2 oz (50 g) fresh breadcrumbs
- salt and black pepper

Serves 4

1. Mix together all of the ingredients for the meatballs in a large bowl, using your hands to bring everything together. Form into small balls, about the size of large walnuts. Place on a tray and put into the refrigerator for at least 30 minutes.

2. Put the tomato sauce into a large pan. Add the meatballs and cook over a medium heat for 20–25 minutes until the meatballs are cooked through. Do not stir until the outer surfaces are cooked so as not to break up the meatballs. Season at the end of cooking with salt and pepper if necessary.

3. Meanwhile, cook the tagliatelle in plenty of boiling water until al dente. Drain the pasta and toss with some of the meatball and sauce mixture, serving the rest on top. Chop the parsley and sprinkle on top.

Tagliatelle Verde with Pesto (v)

Tagliatelle Verde with Pesto (v)

The word "pesto" originates from the Latin root, meaning "to pound, to crush", in reference to the sauce's crushed herbs and garlic.

You will need:
- 2 oz (50 g) fresh basil leaves
- 4 cloves garlic, peeled and chopped
- 2 oz (50 g) pine nuts
- 5 fl.oz (125 ml) olive oil
- 4 oz (100 g) freshly grated Parmesan cheese
- 1 oz (25 g) freshly grated pecorino cheese
- salt and black pepper
- 12 oz (350 g) tagliatelle verde

Serves 4

1. Put the basil leaves, garlic and pine nuts in a blender or food processor with four tablespoons of the olive oil. Blend until smooth, stop the machine and scrape down the sides of the bowl. Blend again while adding the rest of the olive oil in a steady stream, scraping down the sides again. Put into a bowl and mix in the cheeses with a wooden spoon. Season with salt and pepper if necessary.

2. Cook the tagliatelle in plenty of boiling, salted water until al dente. Drain and reserve a few spoonfuls of the cooking liquid. Toss the tagliatelle in the pesto, adding a little of the cooking liquid if necessary.

NB: *If you do not have fresh basil, try making pesto using canned or bottled roasted red peppers. Drain two large peppers and substitute them for the basil in the recipe.*

Tortellini with Fresh Tomato Sauce

Legend has it that tortellini was created in the image of a navel. The timeless combination of cheese and ham, alongside the fresh tomato sauce will have you asking for seconds!

You will need:

- 1 quantity of fresh pasta made with 8 oz (225 g) flour (see p. 11)
- 6 oz (175 g) cooked smoked ham
- 2 oz (50 g) freshly grated Parmesan cheese
- 4 oz (100 g) Gruyère cheese grated
- 2 tbsp fresh parsley
- 1 egg yolk
- 1 quantity of fresh tomato sauce (see p. 21)

Serves 4

1. Wrap the pasta dough in plastic wrap and leave to rest for 30 minutes.

2. Put the ham into a food processor and process until finely ground. Add half the Parmesan, the Gruyère, parsley and egg yolk and process until well mixed together.

3. Cut the dough into four, and using a pasta machine, roll out a piece at a time into a thin sheet. Prepare all of the sheets and cover with plastic wrap to prevent them drying out. Place on to a floured board and cut into 3 in. (7.5 cm) squares. Put a teaspoon of the filling in the center of each square. Moisten the edges with a little water and fold each square diagonally into a triangle. Press the edges together and then curl the two corners together. Repeat using the rest of the dough and filling. Set the finished tortellini aside in the refrigerator loosely covered until ready to cook.

4. Cook the tortellini, a few at a time, for about 3 minutes in plenty of boiling, salted water. Drain and put into a warmed serving dish. Meanwhile, re-heat the tomato sauce and pour over the cooked tortellini. Toss together very gently and serve with the remaining Parmesan cheese.

Tortellini Gratinati (v)

Tortellini Gratinati (v)

Stir the smooth aromatic pesto through this fantastic homemade tortellini—a perfect dish that is suitable for the family or dinner guests!

You will need:
- 1 quantity of fresh pasta made with 8 oz (225 g) flour (see p. 11)
- 8 oz (225 g) ricotta cheese
- 2 tbsp basil or red pepper pesto sauce (see p. 89)
- 3 tbsp fresh parsley
- 3 oz (75 g) butter
- 2 oz (50 g) freshly grated Parmesan cheese
- black pepper

Serves 4

1. Wrap the pasta dough in plastic wrap and leave to rest for 30 minutes.

2. Put the ricotta into a bowl and add the pesto and two tablespoons of parsley. Mix together with a wooden spoon.

3. Cut the dough into four, and using a pasta machine, roll out a piece at a time into a thin sheet. Prepare all of the sheets first, then cover with plastic wrap. Place on to a floured board and cut into 3 in. (7.5 cm) squares. Put a teaspoon of the filling in the center of each square. Moisten the edges with a little water and fold each square diagonally into a triangle. Press the edges together and then curl the two corners together. Repeat using the rest of the dough and filling. Set the finished tortellini aside in the refrigerator loosely covered until ready to cook.

4. Cook the tortellini, a few at a time, for about 3 minutes in plenty of boiling, salted water. Drain well. Melt the butter in a large pan over a low heat. Add the cooked tortellini and toss well. Serve sprinkled with the Parmesan cheese, black pepper and the remaining parsley.

Real Minestrone Soup (v)

Real Minestrone Soup (v)

An Italian staple, minestrone soup was originally intended as a cheap and filling dish, made from leftovers. Today, the soup includes fresh vegetables and is made for its own sake—as a healthy and delicious dish!

You will need:
- 3 tbsp olive oil
- 1 onion finely chopped
- 2 sticks celery, chopped
- 1 large carrot, finely chopped
- 1 zucchini, thinly sliced
- 2 small potatoes, peeled and cut into cubes
- 5 oz (175 g) French beans
- 4 large juicy tomatoes, peeled and chopped
- 14 oz (400 g) canellini or haricot beans
- 30 fl.oz (900 ml) vegetable stock
- 1 bay leaf
- 4 oz (100 g) vermicelli
- 2–3 tbsp pesto (see p. 89)
- salt and black pepper
- 2 oz (50 g) freshly grated Parmesan cheese

Serves 4

1. Heat the olive oil in a large saucepan over a medium heat. Add the onion, celery, carrot and zucchini. Cook for 3–4 minutes and then add the potatoes, French beans and tomatoes. Cook for another 2–3 minutes and then add the canellini or haricot beans with the liquid from the can. Pour over the vegetable stock and add the bay leaf, bring to the boil, lower the heat, cover the pan and simmer gently for 40 minutes.

2. Break the vermicelli into small pieces and add to the soup. Simmer for another 5–6 minutes until the pasta is cooked. Stir in the pesto, season with salt and pepper and serve with the Parmesan cheese.

Conclusion

Hopefully, this book has given you an insight into the wonderful world of pasta. With so many shapes and sizes to choose from, you may well be inspired to cook up a vast array of new and exciting pasta dishes, as well as all the classic favorites.

Whether you're making your own pasta to create a spectacular and complex combination of flavors, or simply eating it with a drizzle of olive oil and shavings of Parmesan, pasta is there to be enjoyed.

Experiment with these dishes and adapt them to suit your tastes. Pasta is a wonderfully versatile food that benefits from a touch of flair and imagination. With this book as a starting point, there is no pasta challenge that you can't respond to! Enjoy, and buon appetito!

Picture Acknowledgements
5-6: Image DJ. 7: Hulton-Deutsch Collection/Corbis.
9: Kevein R.Morris/Corbis. 14: John Hesltine/Corbis.